Shemitah For Christians:

Living in Rhythms of Rest

By Seneca Schurbon

ISBN-13: 978-1-7333795-3-3

DISCLAIMER

The information provided within this book is for general informational purposes only. Even though we have attempted to present accurate information, there are no representations or warranties, express or implied, about the completeness, accuracy, or reliability of the information, products, or services, contained in this book for any purpose. The information is provided "as is," to be used at your own risk.

The information in this book is based on the author's knowledge, experience and opinions. The methods described in this book are not intended to be a definitive set of instructions.

This book is not intended to give financial advice and is sold with the understanding that the author is not engaged in rendering financial or other professional services or advice. If legal or financial advice or other expert assistance is required, the services of a competent professional should be sought to ensure you fully understand your risks.

Table of Contents

Introduction

What if God came up with a system to limit debt, help the poor, the tired, and the over-extended? What if this system also ensured good environmental stewardship? What if we could adapt these principles to our modern society and use it today? That's exactly what we'll be exploring in this book.

God had just pulled ancient Israel out of 400 years of horrific oppression, when He set up these guidelines to rebuild them as a nation and protect them from future calamity. The Shemitah, or "year of release," refers to the seventh year in a cycle where God shares His system for a year-long Sabbath rest and an economic reset. The Shemitah was also the remedy for agricultural problems, wealth disparity, malnutrition, poverty, and burnout.

I believe many of the problems we are facing socially, economically, and environmentally are because we decided we didn't need to follow this seven-year cycle. I also believe that we can bring it down to a personal level to stay in synch with what God is doing and that many of us need the rest and rejuvenation the Shemitah offers. The Shemitah is also a refuge for us during economic downturns, many of which occur during or at the end of Shemitah years.

As in nearly all Jewish traditions, they've added more rigamarole on to what we see God saying in the Bible. This book is an attempt to get back to the basic commands, without all the loopholes and workarounds modern Israel has invented that miss the point of what God is trying to do with our economy, society, and environment.

In the Shemitah year, the land gets to rest, the agricultural society (which was all of Israel at the time) gets to rest, debts are forgiven and slaves go free. Private land gets opened up to all, as do perennial crops.

As in the Israelites early instruction to gather manna every day for five days and gather twice as much on the sixth so they could have a rest day, (Exodus 16:22-27) they were to harvest twice as much food on the sixth year to take the seventh off. (Exodus 23:10-11, Lev 20:18-22)

After seven cycles of seven, there's a Jubilee year, meaning on the fiftieth year, all the Shemitah rules from the forty-ninth year still apply, plus all property reverts back to its original owner or their heirs.

The purpose of the Shemitah year was so the farmland could recover and continue to be a viable place of provision over the long term. So that land could stay in the family and be worth holding on to rather than using it up and moving on. If you lost your land due to debt, you would get it back during the Jubilee year, and it would have rested for the last two years and be ready to go for you.

With a Shemitah year, nobody would get so buried in debt that they would lose all hope. Every seven years was a reset and a new opportunity to make good choices. After debt forgiveness, you could rebuild your life as long as you were willing to make an effort.

The Shemitah makes us aware of our role is as stewards of land and resources. All the earth is the Lord's, and all the money too. To violate the Shemitah should give us pause, is as it effectively says, "This is mine and I won't give it up." The Shemitah ends attachments to materialism, status, and a sense of power over others. The Shemitah allows God to be God.

It allows the wealthy to take time off and reflect, and it allows the poor an escape from crippling debt. It's an opportunity for bettering your situation within the next seven years.

Observing the Shemitah is an act of submission and humility and very often, a big step of faith.

To quit farming with the belief that you'll have enough to eat, have enough income without selling crops, without having loan payments coming in, it's a big step. The Shemitah has the potential to build your faith in God.

There's been a bit of a cop-out that the Shemitah doesn't apply to those of us who are not farmers, financiers, or slave owners. Most of what is being taught is that the Shemitah applies to Jews living in Israel who own land

and are involved in agriculture. The rest of us, and especially Western Christians, don't observe. I don't see where that separation is in the Bible.

Here are my questions: Are you not grafted in? (Romans 11:17) Does God not care about land and societies beyond Israel? Are we then immune to the problems associated with not keeping the Shemitah? Some teach that though America does not have to keep the Shemitah, it's vulnerable to the curses that come with not keeping it. This makes little sense to me. God has always provided opportunities to do the right thing to avoid the bad consequences.

I'm still going to claim grace, but that's because Jesus, not geography. You don't have to observe the Shemitah, but I think it's worth doing, even if only partway. You do it for love — love of your land, love of your community, love of your neighbors and love of God. It's choosing to respect His wisdom and way of keeping things running, and keeping things sustainable.

How Modern Israel
Deals With This

As you can imagine, giving up farming for a year and canceling all loans has major economic consequences. To help relieve some of this, rabbis came up with some ideas. For instance, they decided Jewish farmers could sell their land to non-Jews with an agreement that the land ownership would revert back at the end of the Shemitah year. Then the Jewish farmer could continue to work the land. They could transfer debts to a religious court in order for the debt to survive Shemitah. Similarly, the court may pay the farmers to pick their produce and store it in a place rented by the court. The court then distributes the fruit to the public, passing on the cost of the farmer's labor. Thus, the farmers are not marketing their produce, but still get paid for their labor.

Hydroponics is another method that is used because it doesn't involve the land. As far as eating, they buy produce from Arab farmers, much of it coming from Gaza. There are those who figure that giving money to people that shoot rockets at you is not the best idea.

They came up with all of these ways to follow the letter of the law and completely missed the spirit in which it was intended. These are ways to hold on rather than release and they replace God as provider.

All of this hinges on certain parties being exempt. As you might have picked up, I don't see where the Bible says everyone outside of Israel gets a pass.

More and more Israelis are working their way back to legitimate Shemitah observance. Meanwhile, let's look at what the Bible actually says about how Shemitah works. We'll take it one point at a time.

Five Key Principles
From the Bible

There are five main points made in biblical text regarding the Shemitah and how we are supposed to incorporate it into society. In our case, we'll be looking at these on a much more personal level. Shemitah starts with you! At the end of each principle, I'll ask some questions for you to reflect on how you can incorporate each key into your current lifestyle and give you some space to journal.

1. The Land Rests

"For six years you are to sow your fields and harvest the crops, but during the seventh year let the land lie unplowed and unused."
Exodus 23:10-11.

"The Lord said to Moses at Mount Sinai, 'Speak to the Israelites and say to them: When you enter the land I am going to give you, the land itself must observe a sabbath to the Lord. For six years sow your fields, and for six years prune your vineyards and gather their crops. But in the seventh year the land is to have a year of sabbath rest, a sabbath to the Lord. Do not sow your fields or prune your vineyards. Do not reap what grows of itself or harvest the grapes of your untended vines. The land is to have a year of rest. Whatever the land yields during the sabbath year will be food for you—for yourself, your male and female servants, and the hired worker and temporary resident who live among you, as well as for your livestock and the wild animals in your land. Whatever the land produces may be eaten.'"
Leviticus 25:1-7.

It's a tad confusing at first. Do not reap or harvest, but hey, you can eat. What this means is that you can't commercially harvest, store up, or take to market. If you or others want to glean for yourselves of whatever comes up on its own for a meal, that is perfectly permissible.

And if nobody is growing anything, then how does everybody eat? Here is what God said about that.

> *"Follow my decrees and be careful to obey my laws, and you will live safely in the land. Then the land will yield its fruit, and you will eat your fill and live there in safety. You may ask, 'What will we eat in the seventh year if we do not plant or harvest our crops?' I will send you such a blessing in the sixth year that the land will yield enough for three years. While you plant during the eighth year, you will eat from the old crop and will continue to eat from it until the harvest of the ninth year comes in."*
> Leviticus 25:18-22.

We've seen this before where God gave the Israelites extra manna on the sixth day so that they would not have to gather or cook on the seventh. He also told them it would not spoil, even though it did every other day if they tried to save any.

> God said, "Observe my Sabbaths and have reverence for my sanctuary. I am the Lord. If you follow my decrees and are careful to obey my commands, I will send you rain in its season, and the ground will yield its crops and the trees their fruit. Your threshing will continue until grape harvest and the grape harvest will continue until planting, and you will eat all the food you want and live in safety in your land. I will grant peace in the land, and you will lie down and no one will make you afraid. I will remove wild beasts from the land, and the sword will not pass through your country. You will pursue your enemies, and they will fall by the sword before you. Five of you will chase a hundred, and a hundred of you will chase ten thousand, and your enemies will fall by the sword before you. I will look on you with favor and make you fruitful and increase your numbers, and I will keep my covenant with you. You will still be eating last year's harvest when you will have to move it out to make room for the new. I will put my dwelling place among you, and

I will not abhor you. I will walk among you and be your God, and you will be my people. I am the Lord your God, who brought you out of Egypt so that you would no longer be slaves to the Egyptians; I broke the bars of your yoke and enabled you to walk with heads held high." Leviticus 26:2-13.

To observe, we would let our home gardens or commercial fields rest. For me, I'm canning, freezing and dehydrating in full swing right now. (August) I will stock up on (buy) all the other veggies, flour, and plant-based foods I need for our household. I'll probably prune my blackberry vines before the Shemitah year, and grapes as well, but then let them go. They'll wander over the fence, where the neighbor will pick, and the deer too. In the spring, rhubarb will come up and I'll make pie, but won't freeze any. Any carrots that I left in the ground to harvest throughout the winter will go to seed, and might self-sow unless I mulch the entire area to keep weeds down. I'm not going to count on a volunteer crop of carrots, but that would technically be permissible to eat as are wild foraged crops.

Meat, seafood, dairy, and eggs are still things we can acquire throughout the year.

And there's the grocery store... This is me adding to what God said, but it seems to me, if you're paying someone else to void the Shemitah, you're not really keeping it either. God's plan was for ALL the land to rest. If you're a Christian, you're not under the law, but this still contributes to the condition we're in. You are also missing out on this process and faith walk of God's provision and healing for the land, yet this cycle takes some planning. God didn't spring this on the Israelites in year six. He told them when they didn't even have land yet, so if this is new to you, figure out what you can do, or plan to catch it next round.

Reflection Questions:

1. In an ideal situation, what do you see as the best incorporation of land rest for you? Would it be not planting your own garden for a year? Would it be lots of home-grown food preserving on year six? Would it be purchasing food ahead of time?

2. Is this possible for you now?

3. If not, what steps can you take so that it is possible someday?

4. If it is possible, what do you need to do first?

2. Let the Poor Glean From Your Land

> *"For six years you are to sow your fields and harvest the crops, but during the seventh year let the land lie unplowed and unused. Then the poor among your people may get food from it, and the wild animals may eat what is left. Do the same with your vineyard and your olive grove."*
> Exodus 23:10-11.

It's an interesting consideration for the poor and the wildlife, without really going out of your way for them.

Some people take down their fences. Others merely leave gates open, and I used to take mine down so that deer could get into my garden at the end of the season. For most of us, removing fences is not practical, and often we are fencing pets in rather than everything else out. However, we could take fruit from our trees to the food bank, invite neighbors in need to pick their own, or put some apples over the fence for the deer or neighbors' horses. Even leaving the garden unruly can create shelter and food through the winter for birds and insects.

Reflection Questions:

1. What assets do you have that would otherwise go to waste?

2. How can you help provide food security for other people and wildlife?

3. Forgive Debts

"At the end of every seven years you must cancel debts. This is how it is to be done: Every creditor shall cancel any loan they have made to a fellow Israelite. They shall not require payment from anyone among their own people, because the Lord's time for canceling debts has been proclaimed. You may require payment from a foreigner, but you must cancel any debt your fellow Israelite owes you. However, there need be no poor people among you, for in the land the Lord your God is giving you to possess as your inheritance, he will richly bless you, if only you fully obey the Lord your God and are careful to follow all these commands I am giving you today. For the Lord your God will bless you as he has promised, and you will lend to many nations but will borrow from none. You will rule over many nations but none will rule over you."

"If anyone is poor among your fellow Israelites in any of the towns of the land the Lord your God is giving you, do not be hardhearted or tightfisted toward them. Rather, be openhanded and freely

lend them whatever they need. Be careful not to harbor this wicked thought: 'The seventh year, the year for canceling debts, is near,' so that you do not show ill will toward the needy among your fellow Israelites and give them nothing. They may then appeal to the Lord against you, and you will be found guilty of sin. Give generously to them and do so without a grudging heart; then because of this the Lord your God will bless you in all your work and in everything you put your hand to. There will always be poor people in the land. Therefore I command you to be openhanded toward your fellow Israelites who are poor and needy in your land."

Deuteronomy 15:1-11.

The average person is in debt rather than one who is in a position to forgive them right? Not exactly. Matthew 18, The Parable of the Unmerciful Servant, draws a parallel about unforgiveness in our heart and a debt owed.

I like what Mike Parsons had to say about this in his book *My Journey Beyond Beyond*, "We encourage people to make an invoice to settle the accounts as in the parable. We use a three-column record: in column one, the offense:

what was done or said (words have just as much power as actions, if not more) or what was not done or said. In column two, list what effects or consequences it has had on your life, for example in your relationships, image, or identity. Then column three is how this is affecting you now, today. Once we have made the invoice and recognized the full extent of the debt owed to us, we forgive and release the person from our heart and tear up the invoice (or even burn it) as a practical expression of what we are choosing to do."

Anderick Biddle, in his book *The Shemitah Solution* talks about the Hebrew word for debt *"neshiy"* which not only refers to something owed, but the pictograph can be translated as a continuous pressure. In this sense, it may not be exclusively about monetary debt, but a circumstance that keeps someone under continuous pressure. He goes on to discuss that we should seek to help unburden others and destroy yokes of oppression.

Reflection Questions:

1. Have you loaned any money or tangible goods to anyone that you haven't collected on?

2. If so, can you let it go?

3. Is there anyone you need to forgive? Or maybe you've forgiven them but still feel owed?

4. Are there people in your life that are under pressure? How can you help?

Feel free to copy the next page, tear it out, shred it up, and/or burn it as you see fit.

How it Affects Me Now	Effects and/or Consequences	The Offense

Signature:

Date:

Forgiven

4. Free Slaves

"If any of your people—Hebrew men or women— sell themselves to you and serve you six years, in the seventh year you must let them go free. And when you release them, do not send them away empty-handed. Supply them liberally from your flock, your threshing floor and your winepress. Give to them as the Lord your God has blessed you. Remember that you were slaves in Egypt and the Lord your God redeemed you. That is why I give you this command today."

Deuteronomy 15:12-15.

Slavery is much less common in today's world, but we can enslave people through unforgiveness by making them jump through never-ending hoops in efforts to reconcile or make things right. When what they do can never make up for the debt, there are only two options. Forgive and bless them on the way out the door, or forgive and move forward together with a clean slate. Either way sets both of you free. I unpack another kind of slavery more fully in the "Economic Connection" chapter.

Reflection Questions:

1. Is there anyone in your life where you maintain the upper hand in the relationship? Why is that?

2. Are you keeping someone around because they are useful to you?

3. Do you feel in bondage to anyone? Is it time to declare your own freedom?

5. Gather and Teach

"Then Moses commanded them: 'At the end of every seven years, in the year for canceling debts, during the Festival of Tabernacles, when all Israel comes to appear before the Lord your God at the place he will choose, you shall read this law before them in their hearing. Assemble the people—men, women and children, and the foreigners residing in your towns—so they can listen and learn to fear the Lord your God and follow carefully all the words of this law. Their children, who do not know this law, must hear it and learn to fear the Lord your God as long as you live in the land you are crossing the Jordan to possess.'"

Deuteronomy 31:10-13.

If you do not understand the Shemitah, you will not reap the benefits, and you'll wind up with the consequences. A modern example of this is Juneteenth. They had officially outlawed slavery in the United States, but slaves in Texas didn't know about this for another two-and-a-half years. General Granger had the job of gathering and teaching. US slavery had zero in common with any sort of biblical model, so this is not surprising, but public announcements, like Moses said, were effective. As in any laws, we need to know our rights.

I haven't seen any such town assembly during Festival of Tabernacles to attend, but we can listen to the Bible via audio. We can have Bible studies. We can teach children and others. We can write books. You don't need a large audience, just be obedient to teach what you can to who you can.

Reflection Questions:

1. This was regarding Torah law, but what is a message God has given you that you need to get out there?

2. If so, what format for delivery are you equipped to use? Or maybe even need to learn to use? (Book, YouTube, one-on-one, etc.)

3. Is there a way that you can share the freedom of the gospel, or other biblical principle that will set others free in various areas?

When Is It?

This is not a book that sets any dates of the Shemitah year. There is controversy over which years are Shemitah years, and which is the correct calendar. I follow these alternative calculations, and it would surprise me if the modern Jewish calendar that most people follow is correct. However, I have many personal anecdotes of things happening on feast days, calculated new months, and other events. There are Shemitah stories from others observing or failing to observe and regretting it that time correctly with the mainstream Jewish calendar. Maybe

God in His grace goes along because a sector of society is earnestly trying.

Because so much in my own life syncs with the modern Jewish calendar. I've chosen to follow it, while monitoring alternative calculations and observances.

Be free to observe during the time you feel is right and allow me to do the same.

There is also a debate over whether the Shemitah goes from Tishrei to Tishrei or Nisan to Nisan. Jewish tradition has it starting in Tishrei, on Rosh Hashanah and go to Elul 29. But starting the year in Tishrei is not what God actually said. (Exodus 12:2)

As a Westerner and a gardener, this makes sense to me as Nisan is in the spring and the beginning of the growing season. But Israel sows barley and other crops in late fall. Barley is supposed to ripen in Nisan, so if they went from Nisan to Nisan, they would not have a crop for two and a half years instead of one and a half.

Additionally, I kept getting hung up on Deuteronomy 31:10, "At the end of every seven years in the year for canceling debts, during the festival of Tabernacles."

Tabernacles is in Tishrei, but it's not at the end of the year. If you say Nisan is the first of the year, then it's in the middle. If you say Tishrei is the first of the year, it's at the beginning. The first of Tishrei, though, is "the new year for seasons."

It's believed that Tishrei is the anniversary of creation so they count years up from there. The Feast of Tabernacles certainly would be after the wrap up of the agricultural year. The Feast of Tabernacles is also called The Feast of the Ingathering. They hang samples of fall crops up in makeshift tents to acknowledge God's faithfulness in providing. It's a celebration of provision in the current harvest and a remembrance of His provision and protection in the past. It seems rather fitting for kicking off a seventh year, but probably a bit lack-luster in the eighth, or the first year in the new sabbatical cycle.

By the way, it says in Zechariah 14 that gentile nations in the millennial reign are required to celebrate the Feast of

Tabernacles. So much for that idea that this is only Jewish Israelis.

> *And it shall come to pass, that every one that is left of all the nations which came against Jerusalem shall even go up from year to year to worship the King, the Lord of hosts, and to keep the feast of tabernacles. And it shall be, that whoso will not come up of all the families of the earth unto Jerusalem to worship the King, the Lord of hosts, even upon them shall be no rain. And if the family of Egypt go not up, and come not, that have no rain; there shall be the plague, wherewith the Lord will smite the heathen that come not up to keep the feast of tabernacles.*
> Zechariah 14:16-18.

Tishrei is also the seventh month, which is an appropriate time to begin a Sabbath. I believe Shemitah starts in Tishrei.

Do You Need A Year Off?

Ancient Israel was an agrarian society, meaning almost everybody had something to do with food. The Shemitah had the effect of many people being off work for a year. A question in my mind was whether taking a year off should be a goal for us as well in modern non-agricultural work. After all, we see the Shemitah effects across all sectors of modern society when we have recessions and depressions in a Shemitah year.

We've also woven a strong connection between modern economics and business to the original industry of agriculture. We talk about "sowing and reaping" in a financial sense. We launch new startups with "seed money," we talk about our return on investment as a "yield," and we've always got something coming to "fruition." To "plow back" is to reinvest our earnings or profits in the business. We talk about "breaking new ground" in terms of the effort of moving into a new market. Our work changed, but the language didn't.

My business actually has an agricultural element to it. I manufacture flower essences. These are not the same as essential oils or herbal tinctures, but another form of natural healing (www.freedom-flowers.com). Much of what I use are wildflowers, perennials, or self-sowers. There is no reliance on monoculture fields as if I were an essential oils company or flower farmer. I don't believe it causes any ecological repercussions.

However, there is still an element of harvest to it. I am planning for the business to observe the Shemitah in terms of production. I might scale back on what I do and not start new projects during the Shemitah, so that I can rest as much as possible or have room for spiritual pursuits.

Taking a year is a hard determination to make, but it's easier when you're your own boss. If you're not, and you'd like to keep your job, it might be possible to negotiate an extended leave of absence. Some companies even offer sabbatical leave if you've been with the company enough years. You will of course need to have financially prepared on the other years. If taking that much time off is too much, maybe you can plan ahead to have less responsibilities in other areas. Most of us wind up with too much on our plate by default. We drift straight into it. It takes strong intention and creative thinking to simplify in life.

The weekly Sabbath was made for man. The land doesn't get to rest on a Saturday or Sunday which you might observe. All the weekly Sabbaths between each Shemitah equal out to one Jewish year, and the land gets what you owe it on the seventh. That's the logic that I've been able to ferret out of the Bible.

If you've done a good job of taking your rest days, I wouldn't worry about prepping for a year off, but if you're like many entrepreneurs where you poured yourself into your business every day of the week, working towards a self-sustaining system and taking time off could be a good goal for you. The same goes for those juggling jobs and mountainous personal responsibilities. Working that much is going to catch up with you at some point. And the Shemitah you prepare for and voluntarily observe is much better than the one forced upon you.

To be clear, I don't believe in an angry, spiteful God who punishes people that don't follow the rules. I believe that there are natural consequences of our choices and it's the grace of God that we are protected from them to the extent that we are. Learning to recognize when you have grace to push in an area versus when you need to stop and submit is an invaluable skill in business or life in general.

If you are in business, and would like a Christian resource for building yours on a good foundation, check out my Supernatural Business training at supernaturalbiz.com.

What If We Don't Do Shemitah?

The consequences are as follows:

> "But if you will not listen to me and carry out all
> these commands, and if you reject my decrees and
> abhor my laws and fail to carry out all my
> commands and so violate my covenant, then I will
> do this to you: I will bring on you sudden terror,
> wasting diseases and fever that will destroy your
> sight and sap your strength. You will plant seed
> in vain, because your enemies will eat it. I will set

my face against you so that you will be defeated by your enemies; those who hate you will rule over you, and you will flee even when no one is pursuing you."

"If after all this you will not listen to me, I will punish you for your sins seven times over. I will break down your stubborn pride and make the sky above you like iron and the ground beneath you like bronze. Your strength will be spent in vain, because your soil will not yield its crops, nor will the trees of your land yield their fruit."

"If you remain hostile toward me and refuse to listen to me, I will multiply your afflictions seven times over, as your sins deserve. I will send wild animals against you, and they will rob you of your children, destroy your cattle and make you so few in number that your roads will be deserted. If in spite of these things you do not accept my correction but continue to be hostile toward me, I myself will be hostile toward you and will afflict you for your sins seven times over. And I will bring the sword on you to avenge the breaking of the covenant. When you withdraw into your *cities, I will send a plague among you, and you will be given into enemy hands. When I cut off your supply of bread, ten women will be able to bake your bread in one oven, and they will dole out the bread by weight. You will eat, but you will not be satisfied."*

"If in spite of this you still do not listen to me but continue to be hostile toward me, then in my anger I will be hostile toward you, and I myself will punish you for your sins seven times over. You will eat the flesh of your sons and the flesh of your daughters. I will destroy your high places, cut down your incense altars and pile your dead bodies on the lifeless forms of your idols, and I will abhor you. I will turn your cities into ruins and lay waste your sanctuaries, and I will take no delight in the pleasing aroma of your offerings. I myself will lay waste the land, so that your enemies who live there will be appalled. I will scatter you among the nations and will draw out my sword and pursue you. Your land will be laid waste, and your cities will lie in ruins. Then the land will enjoy its sabbath years all the time that it lies desolate and you are in the country of your

enemies; then the land will rest and enjoy its sabbaths.All the time that it lies desolate, the land will have the rest it did not have during the sabbaths you lived in it."
Leviticus 26:14-35

Like many people, I've struggled with the juxtaposition of the Old Testament wrath and the New Testament Jesus. Writers in the Old Testament believed in the sovereignty of God. Sovereignty, interpreted as everything that ever happens is God's will. I think we all know better. If that were true, Jesus would be in complete rebellion because he went around willy-nilly undoing a lot of things.

Jesus was also quite anti-wrath and judgment. Setting wrath and judgment aside, I believe that there are natural laws set in place and God has given instruction that keeps us from negative consequences when followed. I also believe that God does some economic resets from time to time and that Satan tries to piggyback on to do as much damage as possible. There has been prophecy regarding the Shemitah years, always bringing up the wrath part of the scriptures about the Shemitah. This does not hold up to the standards of New Testament prophecy. Does it edify, build up, encourage, comfort? (1 Corinthians 14:3)

None that I've heard. Shemitah is actually a place of hiddenness. It's a refuge to those who would seek it.

The book *Dirt: The Erosion of Civilization* tracks civilizations throughout history and across multiple continents, and details their fall in correlation with soil stewardship. Once the soil could no longer support the people, they became vulnerable to plagues, invading tribes and famine.

Roman leaders noticed the correlation between poor land practices that resulted in ruined fields and slave labor, or owners that treated land as disposable. They passed laws tying people to the land that they cultivated, rather than passing it off to slave labor. They even made it illegal for a farmer's son to leave the family farm. This was to prop up the problematic agricultural scene that fed the population.

God also seemed to ensure that land stayed in the family with Jubilee law where the longest that land could ever leave your family was forty-nine years. Understanding the generational aspect of land generally produces better stewards.

Roman practices were that of adding manure, using cover crops, living mulches, crop rotation, all things we today see as sustainable. It wasn't enough.

Columella, an authority on Roman agriculture in De Re Rustica, talked about other agricultural writers who said that the land was "exhausted" from its former productivity. He argued this, saying that it couldn't possibly be the case because the gods endowed the land with perpetual fertility. His belief was that the problem was the farmer's treatment of the land.

Historians rightly blame multiple factors why a society collapses. But any civilization's relationship to its land has been a marker of its lifespan. Poor nutrition in the soil leads to poor nutrition in a body. Disease resistance plummets, famine weakens the warriors. You can't stay on a depleted land unless you import all your food. In ancient times, if you pick up and move, it's risky. You are not established in a new land. You do not have your walled city. There's a vulnerability that comes with migration. Taking care of your land is worth the effort.

Economic Connections

There have been other teachers that have pointed out the correlations between all the major depressions and recessions in the United States and Shemitah years. They've done a fine job compiling that data, and I don't want to reinvent the wheel or go down the judgement rabbit hole.

I will say that the data is hard to brush off as coincidental. Now that you understand what the Shemitah is, you can see it operating in our day and society. Think about what happened when ancient Israel stopped farming and set people free of their debt.

When we see a Shemitah operating in modern times, there are similar markers that we can look for. Production slows down or stops, unemployment goes up, businesses close, bankruptcies are filed, foreclosures happen. It doesn't happen every Shemitah. Israel got away with not observing it for 490 years. (2 Chronicles 36:21)

The end of the Shemitah year is more dramatic than the onset. Not much changes in the beginning. Crops are wrapping up anyway, it's just that no more are sown. Living off the past season is standard practice. Things slow down a bit, but no big whoop. All the brouhaha is at the end when the slaves are freed and debts forgiven.

Slavery is not a thing of the past. Remember, Proverbs 22:7 says the borrower is slave to the lender. Today, there isn't such a direct line. Nowadays it's called having a job, or two, or three to make ends meet. A large sector of society is in debt, and just barely getting by. Many are working very hard and cannot get traction and get ahead in life.

I believe we should all be working in some form, but there's a big difference between contributing in a way in which you're called, being able to own assets and build towards something, and being run ragged in a dead-end job having all your money leave faster than it comes in.

We have had predatory irresponsible lenders charging high interest rates and letting people take on more debt than they should. If a loan never went longer than seven years, wouldn't the lender be more conservative in how much they loan and to whom? It seems to me that would be the case.

We have a verse warning us about stinginess, (Deuteronomy 15:9) but I doubt that applies to helping somebody buy a new sports car. There's a lot to be said for personal responsibility here. Lenders are not the only problem. Even you can choose not to get into a loan that takes you beyond the seventh year. Better yet, don't go into debt at all.

If God in His wisdom sees a country spiraling out of control with debt, slavery in the form of overwork, and He performs an economic reset, I believe he'll do it in a Shemitah year, and those who prepared for it will come through it in good shape, or at least better off than those who aren't keeping the Sabbath year.

In 2007-2008, I did not know of the Shemitah, but I did know God. And I got a great financial tip early in the year. I had about $140,000 in the stock market and I heard to move my money. I got percentages of how much to put where and the result was some very conservative investments. Not my style at all. I made my money by investing in the most speculative, risky things that I could find. I was eighteen when I started investing, and I owned nothing but a $500 car, so I had nothing to lose. It was easier to keep that attitude than shift it, so I believe God intervened here. I was told to let those allocations ride until fall. Hmmm, fall like autumn? Fall of the market? Fall of civilization?

Fall 2008 is when the housing crisis hit. Borrowers defaulted on loans, the stock market crashed, the US government bailed out Wall Street, and I was okay. We owned our home outright, and I lost a few thousand, while many people took a very hard hit. When I supposed it bottomed out, I started dumping as much money as I could scrape together back into the market. As soon as I did, I heard a voice say, "You are going to be so, so happy you did that."

It was a Shemitah year, and I prepared but I didn't store food.

Following the letter of the law is not a substitute for listening to God and being able to recognize his voice in many forms. As I write this in mid 2021 there are many people with no knowledge of the Shemitah with that feeling in their bones that they need to store food. If we can pay attention to the cycles and check in with God, we can be led by the Spirit and not the law.

The following Shemitah, 2017, everybody was on high alert with Jonathan Kahn's Shemitah book out talking about economic collapse on Shemitah years. 2008 was still fresh in everyone's mind. People were telling me to pull my money out. I tuned into God, wasn't feeling it, and did nothing in preparation that year. Currently, I observe more fully and traditionally, but it's not out of fear of what will happen. Fear is a terrible decision maker. God doesn't give us a spirit of fear, follow the peace. (2 Timothy 1:7)

Observing all the feasts are practice. Yes, I'm about to compare the Shemitah to a feast. In Leviticus 23:2, "Speak to the Israelites and say to them: 'These are my appointed festivals, the appointed festivals of the LORD, which you are to proclaim as sacred assemblies.'" The words "sacred assemblies" in Hebrew mean rehearsals! Many have taught that the feasts are dress rehearsals for future events. Indeed, they are foreshadowing of the return of Jesus, the binding of Satan, the rule of the Kingdom of God on earth, and the resurrections. While man's holidays are memorials and a time of honor, God's holidays are that and then some. They are divine appointments, and we do not know exactly what is in store each time one comes around. You need to show up to find out! Those who made a practice of going to Jerusalem every year for Shavuot were the ones that were in the right place at the right time to receive the first outpouring of the Holy Spirit. (Deut. 16:16, Acts 2:1-4)

I view the Shemitah the same way. While not a feast, it is tied to them, and God first discusses it in the same conversation when He lays out the feast times and customs (Exodus 23). It is part of the cycle. The Shemitah and the feasts are designed to have you operating in a certain way at a certain time, so that God can do a thing, and you'll benefit. The Shemitah should not provoke hand wringing and doom and gloom, which seems to be a recent thing in Christian circles.

The Shemitah comes with many blessings for those who are prepared, and it takes time to get into the rhythm, especially in a society with a belief system that has ignored it. If you are doing what you're supposed to be doing, then you'll be in the right place at the right time.

Keep in mind, God never expected His people to suddenly fall right into step with this. If this is new to you, just learn for now and do the steps that you find reasonable or resonate with you. The Israelites had decades of advance notice before they had to put it all into practice.

Shemitah for Christians: Living in Rhythms of Rest

Stocking Up

The most obvious thing we face is how are we going to eat if we stop growing food or buying food that was grown in a Shemitah year? On the timeline of human history, we're actually not that far removed from when people stocked food to get through until the next harvest. It's absolutely doable to store food from a non-Shemitah year, IF you prepare to do so.

God saw this question coming.

"You may ask, 'What will we eat in the seventh year if we do not plant or harvest our crops? I will send you such a blessing in the sixth year that the land will yield enough for three years. While you plant during the eighth year, you will eat from the old crop and will continue to eat from it until the harvest of the ninth year comes in."

Leviticus 25:20-22.

Remember that this applies to crops, not meat, dairy and seafood, and you can still find fresh food outside, just not in stores. However, if you are expecting an economic hit, storing meat and dairy might be wisdom. For a typical non-catastrophic Shemitah, which will be most of them, you're just giving the land a break if it's your land, and you're not contributing to the national and international soil depletion problems with your dollars.

If you garden, you might already be in the swing of putting up whatever you have in surplus. Still, to skip a year is probably a stretch. Most people are not stocked up beyond a week or two. Having to look at a year plus waiting for the crop to come in is pretty intimidating. I would advise sticking as close to what you normally eat as possible. If you eat a lot of salads that will be tough. There are forageable greens and they can be much healthier than lettuce, but they have their own flavors and they won't be the same as what you're used to. Greens powder can be helpful for making sure you're still getting the health benefits of deep green leafy vegetables.

Some people make a weekly menu and times that by fifty-two. I need more variety than that, particularly because we make a lot of something and eat it for a few days. Therefore, I have a monthly menu. If I eat spaghetti once a month, I need about eighteen jars of sauce and half that of noodles.

That's to get through about a year and a half. I will then purchase all this on sale close to or after the beginning of the Shemitah year. (Yes, I still shop after the first of the new year, because what's on the market is a previous year's crop.) If I have volunteer tomatoes coming up, and I probably will, then I can sauce some of those during the summer of the Shemitah and stretch my stock out a bit. Remember, you can pick and eat, just don't get into a whole canning session.

Figure out what it takes to make all the meals you like, how much you will need and go shopping. You'll want an overage of staples so you can make other things on a whim. Consider all your holidays as well. Canned goods should hold fine for that length of time, frozen veggies and fruit can go about eight to twelve months, freeze-dried food is good from ten to twenty-five years, though only a year after you open the container. You can buy number ten cans of basic freeze-dried fruits and vegetables, and even full meals, though those are not as economical or versatile as ingredients.

Shopping farm stands and talking to the growers can help you discover onion, apple, pear, and winter squash varieties with the longest storage life. I have no trouble keeping my onions a year though I like pre-diced and freeze-dried so I don't have to get out a knife, cutting board, and cry every time I want onion in something.

Dehydrated foods can easily last the timeframe of the Shemitah if done properly. The best use of dried vegetables is soups and stews where they can have a long cook time and a lot of liquid. An advantage of dehydration is that it shrinks everything down to save on storage space. My favorite things to have dehydrated, even on a non Shemitah year, are celery, onions, and black-bean flakes for fast refried beans. Mangoes, apricots, and pineapple are my favorite fruits, although any fruits are good to throw into homemade granola. Store some rolled oats as well!

You can repackage many things in glass jars or Mylar bags that are vacuum sealed or have an oxygen absorber tossed in. Oxygen shortens the life of food, so by either vacuum sealing or using the oxygen absorbers, you can have it last past the "best by" date.

You can put white flour in a Mylar bag with an oxygen absorber, and then in a five-gallon bucket. For wheat flour, it's best to grind wheat as you need it because it goes rancid regardless of what you do, unless you freeze it. Brown rice goes rancid within a few months, but not parboiled brown rice! White rice lasts indefinitely. Other things you might want to repackage are grains, pasta, crackers, cereal, and snack foods.

All plastic is porous. Ziplock bags are the worst storage container, food grade buckets aren't too bad, but they still let some air in. Everything else made of plastic falls somewhere in between.

You'll need to decide whether you want to go with jars or mylar for the best storage options. I use both on a case-by-case basis. I like jars, but for voluminous things like flour and large amounts of things, mylar comes in many sizes, including five-gallon bags.

You'll want to make sure you're buying no less than seven ml Mylar so that it holds up well. You'll also need to use an appropriately sized oxygen absorber with it. It's not recommended to vacuum seal mylar because the bags are fragile and get holes from the food being drawn too tightly. Many people store larger quantities in five-gallon Mylar bags and put the bags inside a bucket. The bucket prevents against holes, mice, etc.

You need to heat seal Mylar bags. You can do that with an iron or I use a hair straightener. A curling iron would be fine too.

As far as oxygen absorbers, use the right size for the container you've got. Most places that sell them have that information available. They are inexpensive, and it's better to buy ten packs of ten than one pack of a hundred. This is because once you open them, you have a matter of minutes to get them where they need to go and get them sealed up. They absorb oxygen and create a deficiency in a sealed environment, but if they are out absorbing their capacity from your room, then they can't suck any more out of your bag or jar. Work fast and seal up any leftovers. If you're packing a lot of containers, it's best to get them all ready at once and have someone coming along behind you putting lids on jars or sealing bags after you put the absorbers in.

Preserving Fresh Food

Freezing, canning, dehydrating, freeze drying, root cellaring, and fermenting are the main ways to preserve food. The best is to do some combination of most of the above. Your personal tastes, lifestyle, dietary requirements, and resources available all dictate how you're going to get this done.

Root cellaring is probably the simplest one once you figured out what to put where. If you have an actual root cellar, you're probably already storing crops. If you don't, you may have an overlooked area that's a suitable match for certain types of crops. An unheated room in your house, an outbuilding with a cooler full of sand, a buried trash can, or even leaving root crops in the ground with bags of fall leaves on top of them, can be just fine. Winter squash keeps easily at household temperatures, and I keep onions and garlic in our main living space as well, although we keep our home on the cool side in the winter.

Crops that need to be keep cold and moist (32-40 degrees F, 90-95 percent humidity are most root crops and tubers, celery, apples, grapes, oranges, pears and cabbage. I've dug carrots and stored in damp sand in coolers, but I much prefer leaving them in the ground in my zone seven garden with some mulch on top, usually bags of leaves. Cold? Check. Moist? Check.

Crops that need to be cool (40-50 degrees F) and moist (85-90 percent humidity) are cucumbers, peppers, melons, eggplant and ripe tomatoes.

Crops that need to be cool and dry (35-40 degrees and 60-70 percent humidity) are garlic and onions.

Getting warmer (50-60 degrees) and 60-70 percent humidity, you can keep pumpkins, winter squash, sweet potatoes.

There's some wiggle room here. Your storage might not be quite what it needs to be, but you can still keep food a while under less-than-optimal conditions. Protection from freezing is probably the biggest thing.

Fermenting is a highly healthy form of preservation, but it's not without a learning curve. Pickles, sauerkraut, and kimchi are the usual things that we think of, but there's a whole range of things that you can ferment. You might try your hand at apple scrap vinegar to get your feet wet. (Google it)

Freeze drying has only recently become an option for households. A freeze dryer is both a big investment and a major appliance, but the food storage life and quality is unparalleled. It also retains 97% of the nutrients in the food that you dry. You can store freeze dried food up to twenty-five years. Freeze-dried foods rehydrate more easily than dehydrated foods. To make the investment work, you need to think in terms of zero waste. Leftovers you can't eat before it goes bad? Freeze dry it. Going on a trip and don't want to eat out? Eat your freeze-dried leftovers. Right now in my fridge I have pepper jack cheese that will go bad before I finish it. So I'll freeze dry the slices. What you shouldn't freeze dry is fatty meat, at least if you want to keep it a long time. Save that for canning or the freezer.

The learning curve is really only what you like and don't like, as well as whether you soak, steam, or spritz each thing to bring it back to proper eating. As far as prep, you put stuff on a tray, put the trays in the dryer and turn it on. You'll get lots of ideas in freeze drying social media groups.

As much as I love my freeze dryer, I still run an old school dehydrator. I like to eat chewy fruit. If I don't have it, I wind up buying gummy candy. And I also think my raisins are way better than the brand names. Let's not forget fruit leather and jerky!

Canning is labor intensive. My rule of thumb is not to can anything I can buy cheap, rather, I turn the produce into a specialty product. It's 2021 and a pack of lids ranges from five to seven dollars. I can buy a can of tomato sauce for fifty cents. It takes a lot of tomatoes, and a lot of work to make a little bit of sauce, but decent salsa costs quite a bit of money, IF you can even find the quality that you want. So that's where I put my tomatoes and effort. Canning soups, stews and chili are all much more worthwhile endeavors than canning their ingredients alone.

Freezing is pretty straightforward. Most vegetables need to be blanched before freezing, but it's simple and frozen vegetables taste great. You can extend the life of your frozen vegetables and fruits by vacuum sealing them in the special bags that come with your sealer.

Here are some resources that I found helpful:

A Year Without the Grocery Store by Karen Morris. More of a prepper focus but really practical and simple ways to get your food storage sorted.

Root Cellaring: The Simple No-Processing Way to Store Fruits and Vegetables by Mike and Nancy Bubel

Ball Blue Book Guide to Preserving (Canning, always go with the latest edition for the most up-to-date safety information.)

Freeze drying is a new frontier. At the time of writing, there isn't a book, but "John in Bibs" on YouTube, and online communities of freeze-drying people will get you off and running.

Foraging and Gleaning

Whatever grows on its own is fair game. That includes not only crops that self-sowed or are perennial, but also lots of wild foods available for fresh food amidst all of our preserved stock. Wild greens, herbs, berries, nuts, seeds, even grains are growing in every untended bit of soil, and learning to use these can be its own art form.

Look for books, especially those specific to regions, with clear color photos that are very helpful. The app "Seek" by INaturalist is helpful as well. Either way, you still need a basic understanding of botany to verify if the app or your book-based ID is indeed correct. For instance, Wild Angelica looks a lot like Water Hemlock. One is medicinal, the other is lethal. The way you know the difference is by whether the veins on the leaves go to the tips, or to the notches. I don't trust an app to make that distinction, but an app can give you a place to begin research. *Botany in a Day* is a supplemental book that you can use to help you determine a correct identification.

Foraged foods can be some of the highest nutrition available. If they were commercially farmed, they would be heavily promoted as "superfoods" but since they have a hard time monetizing weeds, you don't hear about it.

Many invasive plants are edible, meaning our eating becomes a service to the environment. Learning a bit about what's invasive and what's at risk is a good thing. As a general rule, Shemitah year or not, you shouldn't take over 10% from an area. If it's a threatened species, you shouldn't take any. If it's invasive harvest freely.

Another consideration is how you can promote more of a non-invasive plant in the future. With wild mushrooms, a responsible way to harvest is to use mesh bags or loose weave baskets that help distribute the spores. If you're harvesting roots, wait until the plant has gone to seed first. Understanding these things maintains the spirit of Shemitah and helps maintain wild plant populations for the future.

I would encourage you to learn to forage early, and start working these foods into your diet ahead of time, so that you learn how you like them prepared, where you can go to get them, and the times of year they are available. It takes time and experimentation with some of these new flavors.

If you can, find local classes that do field trips, herb walks, or just friends in the know who will let you tag along. In case it hasn't been beaten into you by the time you were three, do not put unknown berries or any other plant parts in your mouth!

Confidence comes in two stages of foragers: The beginning ones who don't know what they don't know, so they think they are always correct, and the ones who have been at it long enough to understand and navigate all the look-alikes. You will not begin in year seven and reach the confidence level of the second person in the same season. Everything is edible. Some things are only edible once.

Gleaning is actually still a thing! People get permission to go through a farm field after it's been mechanically harvested and pick up what's left. By Shemitah rules, all the land is open for anyone to pick, but in our society you better get permission first.

Fallingfruit.org is a worldwide database compiled by people who share their picking spots. I opened up the entry closest to me and it said "Many cherry trees here, not on private land." Jackpot!

There are also organized teams of volunteers that will pick fruit orchards and take the fruit to the food bank. This is more in keeping with what the Shemitah is about, opening up cropland for the poor to gather food. If you'd like to get involved, you can check nationalgleaningproject.org in the US, or feedbackglobal.org in the UK, but that is not the only way to do it.

Activities For Each
Year in the Cycle

By now you understand you can't just decide you're doing Shemitah on Rosh Hashanah of year seven. At least not to its fullest extent. There needs to be preparation time.

If you're familiar with Arthur Burk's teaching on redemptive gifts, these years do indeed follow the fractal of seven. It's unnecessary to understand any of that, but if you already do, I'm sure you'll come up with additional things to do.

Year One: Newness. After the seventh year of downtime and revelation, you probably have new things to put in motion. New paradigms, new solutions and the external chaos are your chess board. Think about what you can start now that will produce in year six. Be that in business or the garden. In the agricultural world, it would be fruit trees since God said you can't eat of them until the fifth year.

> *"When you enter the land and plant any kind of fruit tree, regard its fruit as forbidden. For three years you are to consider it forbidden; it must not be eaten. In the fourth year all its fruit will be holy, an offering of praise to the Lord. But in the fifth year you may eat its fruit. In this way your harvest will be increased. I am the Lord your God."*
>
> Leviticus 19:23-25

Even the secular world knows that if you pull fruit forming on a young tree, it will help the tree grow instead of expending energy to ripen fruit and set seed. Therefore, a bigger harvest in the long run.

Year Two: Exercise spiritual authority over land. Cleansing, speaking blessings along with the basic tending and maintenance.

Year Three: Establish some perennial foods like berries, rhubarb, asparagus, herbs, and Jerusalem artichokes, so you have some fresh food for the Shemitah year. Consider planting day neutral strawberries so that you get a smaller amount over a long season for fresh eating rather than a whopper crop in June. Think about early, mid-season, and late staggered blueberry bushes. Test new crops to see what works well for you and what doesn't. Learn seed saving.

Year Four: Build community. Get to know other local people so you can be a resource for them and vice versa. Don't just shop online, get out and at least peruse local stores so that you know what's there. Attend meetups, take classes and make a point of being involved in the community.

Year Five: Identify things you think you'll want to have if you're doing a year of not buying plant-based groceries. Are you going to grow your own food, or are you buying? If you are going to be doing any kind of preserving, what kind of equipment are you missing? Make a list and start looking for deals. If you need to work on your storage areas, or buy additional shelving, put that on the list too.

Year Six: It's go time! You'll want to look at what your resources are. God said if you were gonna do this, you would get such an abundance in the sixth year, it would carry you through to the eighth.

> *"I will send you such a blessing in the sixth year that the land will yield enough for three years. While you plant during the eighth year, you will eat from the old crop and will continue to eat from it until the harvest of the ninth year comes in."*
> Leviticus 25:21-22.

Not everyone's supply comes as crops these days, so look at what that is for you. Where your abundance is, is probably a clue for what you should rest in year seven. Abundance generally takes stewarding, so put your attention there, whatever that looks like. It's time to watch sales and stock up on food.

Year Seven: The only thing I haven't touched on earlier in this book is that in year seven, if you're a gardener, you're still going to buy your seeds as if you were planting a garden. This is because you'll be getting season six's seeds instead of waiting until year one to purchase the crop from a Shemitah year. Glass jars with new canning lids or mylar bags without oxygen absorbers placed in either the refrigerator or the freezer are the best protection, though most seeds will be fine with no special treatment. I like to group mine by sowing time. Early spring greens vs summer stuff. That way, I'm not getting all of them out and putting them back, causing them to go through more temperature fluctuations than necessary.

At any point in the cycle, I would recommend a soil test, and better yet, reading The Intelligent Gardener: Growing Nutrient Dense Food by Steve Solomon to understand soil remineralization on a deeper level, to understand the rock and the hard place that commercial farmers are in, and why growing organic isn't enough.

Steward your own little patch well.

Shemitah for Christians: Living in Rhythms of Rest

Where To Go From Here

Now that you know what's entailed in the Shemitah, all that's left is to decide how deep into this you need to go. What are you hearing or feeling you need to do? Adherence to the law without the Spirit leaves you with legalism.

Are you going to give your home garden a break? Are you going deeper and take a stand for the land while also making sure you'll be eating good in an economic downturn? Are you going to let that cordless drill you loaned go? Are you going to not only forgive offensive action but also cancel anything you perceive the offender owes you? Is there a way you can help the poor with food security? Can you scale back on activities in favor of spiritual pursuits?

All the above are in tune with what God intends for year seven in the cycle. The Shemitah challenges us on so many levels. Ultimately, it reminds us that God is our source of provision, and we are stewards of His resources. Perhaps every seven years, we need to come back and ground that into our personal experience.

Have you ever considered there might be a pattern to seemingly random "windows of opportunity"? Or that there are specific times where you can be more easily healed or become free in a certain area? If you want to engage with these rhythms throughout each year rather than just every seven years, check out my book Healing in the Hebrew Months: Prophetic Strategies Hidden in the Tribes, Constellations, Gates and Gems.

We have been given an actionable template for our lives and spiritual walk. Moreover, this template has confirmed itself for millennia in the stars, tribes, gates of Jerusalem and the history of each month.

In each Hebraic month you'll discover:

- The area of healing most accessible at that time
- The action needed on your part
- God's intention for you in your current situation
- The warfare tactics that are likely to come up
- How to trade the obstacle for opportunity
- The redemptive purpose of the constellations and gemstones

Healing in the Hebrew Months: Prophetic Strategies Hidden in the Tribes, Constellations, Gates, and Gems is the second book in the life-changing *Healing in the Hebrew Months* series. If you like easy-to-follow action plans, deep explorations of Biblical significance, and knowing where to put your focus for the biggest results, then you'll love my cosmically-aligned guide.

Buy *Healing in the Hebrew Months* to move towards God's promises for you today!
http://mybook.to/hhm

Other Recommended Reading:

Miracles and Dedication: Christian Devotions for the Festival of Lights

The complete *Healing in the Hebrew Months* book series

Links and more information available at:
www.HealingintheHebrewMonths.com

About the Author

Seneca Schurbon

Seneca Schurbon, an author in the Healing in the Hebrew Months series, is an avid explorer of Hebraic time cycles. Her favorite activities are diving into ancient texts, dodging legalism, and kicking around hard questions with friends. She grows extensive gardens, and likes to hang out with her husband at their Idaho home where they discuss how cute their dog is. Outside her books, you can find her getting down to business bringing spirituality to work with natural remedies at www.freedom-flowers.com, and teaching business classes at www.supernaturalbiz.com.

Other Books
by the Author

Healing in the Hebrew Months: Prophetic Strategies Hidden in the Tribes, Constellations, Gates, and Gems

The cyclical patterns of time carry imprints of the past, positive and negative. If you've ever noticed that a certain time of year is always difficult for you, you've experienced this. We can lean into past victories and the feast days to carry the positive forward for our own lives and pull in the opposite direction of the negative dates in history so that we don't add strength and agreement to those outcomes. The more we do this, the stronger those patterns become. Healing in the Hebrew Months offers you a way to become more intentional about understanding these patterns and developing effective strategies to move forward.

The explanations behind each Hebrew month, the original meaning of the corresponding constellations, the tribes that correlate to each, and the Gates of Jerusalem all come together to give us strategy throughout the year. Healing in the Hebrew Months reveals and aligns blessings, areas of healing, potential pitfalls, and warfare to propel you into your destiny.

Supernatural Business: Inviting the Power of God Into the Marketplace

Want to see the supernatural power of God manifest in your business? Want your clients and customers to have a result they can't get from someone else? Learn how a "Kingdom first" focus can take your business places you never imagined.

In Supernatural Business: Inviting the Power of God into the Marketplace, you'll get practical steps to:

- Incorporate the miraculous, whether you're a product or service-based business
- Tap into flow, connections, and needed resources
- Supernatural time phenomena
- Market your business in a way that you can feel great about
- Eliminate self-sabotage and limiting beliefs with helpful tools

You'll also get free admission to our online class with videos and downloadable worksheets, though this book is complete on its own. If you want to see God move in your business in out of the box ways, grab your copy and start taking the limits off your business today!

Flower Power: Essences that Heal

is a practical guide that reveals the power of flower essences to heal emotional imbalances in humans (and their pets!).

Flower essences can help you move past fears and self-limiting beliefs, work through trauma, propel you to achieve your goals, improve your relationships, diffuse stress, anxiety, **and** anger; contribute to healthy spiritual development, and much, much more!

With compelling, intuitive information on more than 100 flower essences and sections addressing trauma, physical healing, and fulfilling your destiny, this handy guide will help you embrace and employ the potential of flower frequencies to help restore the balance and symmetry of a robust, vibrant and satisfying life.

Body Coaching: Losing Weight Through Positive Self-talk

"Body, we need to talk…"

What we say to ourselves and about ourselves matters. Body coaching is a 30-day program of positive self-talk. Taking authority in our spirits over our bodies and giving ourselves the pep talks we've desperately needed.

It's not about will powering your way through another diet or exercise program, it's about partnering your body, mind, and spirit together so that you can experience the breakthroughs you've been longing for.

SENECA SCHURBON, DIANE MOYER, MICHAEL C. KING, MATT EVANS, SAM R. BREWSTER & RUBY HUNTER

BROKEN TO WHOLE

INNER HEALING FOR THE FRAGMENTED SOUL

Broken to Whole: Inner Healing for the Fragmented Soul

Why Aren't You Healed?

Do you ever feel like you continually struggle with certain emotions? Maybe you've tried counseling or various ministries, yet no matter what you do, nothing works.

If traditional prayer and deliverance hasn't cut it, you might be dealing with soul fragments. When we experience a traumatizing event, part of our coping strategy is to wall off a little piece of ourselves in order to contain that emotion. We then go on with life. A fragment is that part of you that's been locked away, inaccessible to healing, until now.

This book is a game-changer in how you'll look at inner healing. We aren't going to beat the drum for repentance and forgiveness although those are beneficial and necessary. Instead, we have made every effort to tell you something you don't know so that you can fill in your missing pieces.

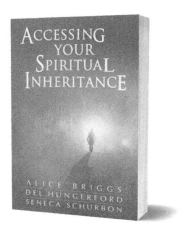

Accessing Your Spiritual Inheritance

It's Your Turn to Go Through the Door

Alice didn't fall down a rabbit hole but she did walk through a mystical doorway in a vision to recover blessings her ancestors failed to claim. When Alice came back and shared her experience, Seneca wasted no time going through her own door. Del's approach differed -- she wound up floating along in her bloodstream!

Through the map we give in our stories, others went through their own doors, leading to better relationships with God, increase in finances, favor, and giftings. Although this book touches on generational curses and how to remove them, we focus on claiming the blessings your family line has lost. However, you'll need to be open to having a vision, and we'll walk you through the step-by-step process of learning to see, so that you, too, can restore your lost generational blessings.
Your hidden inheritance awaits!

Made in the USA
Middletown, DE
09 April 2022